Katie Chin's

Global Family COOKBOOK

**Internationally-Inspired Recipes
Your Friends and Family Will Love!**

TUTTLE Publishing

Tokyo | Rutland, Vermont | Singapore

CONTENTS

Welcome to My Global Family Table! 8
Foreword by Margaret McSweeney 12
My World Pantry Primer 14
Techniques for Cooking Globally 25
Tips on Tools and Utensils 29

Global Go-to Sauces You Need to Know
Chimichurri Sauce 32
Gochujang Sauce 33
Korean BBQ Sauce 33
Thai Peanut Sauce 34
Lemongrass Curry 34
Miso Butter Sauce 35
Lemony Basil Pesto 35

FAMILY DINNERS FOUR WAYS 36

Taco My Tuesday
Cuban Fish Tacos with Citrus Mango Slaw 38
Banh Mi Street Tacos 39
Verde Chicken Tacos 40
Asian Ginger Pork Tacos 41

Doesn't Have to Be Just Another Meatless Monday
Crispy Tofu with Orange Glaze 42
Vegan Mac and Cheese 43
Tofu Mushroom Stir-fry 44
Oven Baked Eggplant Parmesan 45

Mama Mia Make Some Pizza
Cherry Tomato & Basil Pizza on Cauliflower Crust 46
Pepperoni Arugula Sheet Pan Pizza 47
Chicken Tikka Masala Pizza 48
Thai-style Pizza 49

Slammin' Sliders
Honey BBQ Pork Bao Sliders 50
Salmon Sliders with Chipotle Mayo 51
Korean Fried Chicken Sliders 52
Cuban Sliders 53

RISE & SHINE 54
Mexicali Breakfast Skillet 56
Po Po's Chinese Rice Porridge 57
African Eggs Poached in Tomato Sauce 58
Coconut Pancakes with Mango Lime Purée 59
Berry Quinoa Breakfast Bowl 60
Brioche French Toast 61
Breakfast Quinoa Bowl with Chicken Apple Sausage 62
Margaret's Salsa Sunrise Eggs Benedict 62
German Pancake 63

GET THE PARTY STARTED! FINGER FOOD & SMALL BITES 64
Potato Beef Empanadas 66
Pizza Wontons 67
Greek-style Nachos 68
Mini Chicken Samosas with Cilantro Mint Sauce 69
Charred Shishito Peppers 70
Spanish Tapas-style Meatballs 71
Chinese BBQ Bite-size Spare Ribs 72
Bacon, Date & Goat Cheese Potstickers 73
Honey Sriracha Turkey Lollipops 74
Galina's Russian Meatballs 75
Lemongrass Beef Skewers 76
Touchdown Chili Garlic Chicken Wings 77